Brazil

ANDRÉ LICHTENBERG

RSVP
RAINTREE
STECK-VAUGHN
PUBLISHERS
A Steck-Vaughn Company

Austin, Texas

www.steck-vaughn.com

WE COME FROM

Brazil • China • France
Germany • India • Jamaica • Japan
Kenya • Nigeria • South Africa

The family you are about to meet live in a town called Florianópolis. Like any other country, Brazil has many different lifestyles. People live in the country, as well as in towns and cities.

Cover: Lucas and his friends with surfboards and sandboards at the beach
Title page (top to bottom): The Amazon River and the rain forest; *gauchos* in the state of São Paulo; a colorful parrot from the rain forest; a shop selling traditional goods from northern Brazil; traditional boats at Fortaleza in the northeast
Contents page: People enjoying themselves on a beach in northeast Brazil
Index: Lucas by the water in Florianópolis

Published by Raintree Steck-Vaughn Publishers, an imprint of Steck-Vaughn Company

Picture Acknowledgments: Sue Cunningham 15; Edward Parker 18 (lower); South American Pictures/Tony Morrison 14 (top); Tony Stone/John Starr 29 (bottom right); Wayland Picture Library/Tony Morrison title page (second from top), 7, 8 (lower). All the other photographs in this book were taken by André Lichtenberg. The map artwork on page 5 is by Peter Bull.

Library of Congress Cataloging-in-Publication Data
Lichtenberg, André.
Brazil / André Lichtenberg.
    p.   cm.—(We come from)
    Includes bibliographical references and index.
    Summary: Introduces the land, climate, people, and culture of Brazil.
    ISBN 0-8172-5514-1
    1. Brazil—Juvenile literature.
    [1. Brazil.]
    I. Title. II. Series.
    F2508.5.L53 2000
    981—dc21   99-14210

Printed in Italy. Bound in the United States.
1 2 3 4 5 6 7 8 9 0 03 02 01 00 99

Contents

Welcome to Brazil!

"My name is Lucas. Here I am with my parents and Renato."

Lucas Ribeiro is ten years old. He lives with his parents and his brother, Renato, who is thirteen. The family lives in a town on a small island off the southern coast of Brazil. The town is called Florianópolis. You can see where it is on the map on page 5.

▲ From left to right: Mrs. Ribeiro, Renato, Mr. Ribeiro, and Lucas

▶ *Brazil's place in the world*

▼ *Brazil is the largest country in South America.*

Equator

ATLANTIC OCEAN

Manaus

Amazon River

Brasília

N

Rio de Janeiro
São Paulo

Tropic of Capricorn

Florianópolis

| 0 | 200 | 400 | 600 | 800 km |
| 0 | 100 | 200 | 300 | 400 | 500 miles |

BRAZIL

Capital city	Brasilia
Land area	3.3 million sq. mi.
	(8.5 million sq. km)
Population	160 million people
Main language	Portuguese
Main religion	Christianity

5

The Land and Weather

Brazil is a huge country—it covers most of South America. Most Brazilians live along the east coast. The Amazon River, one of the biggest rivers in the world, flows across the northern part of the country.

▲ *In Manaus, houses are built on stilts along the edge of the Amazon River.*

▼ *These children live in a tropical area of northern Brazil.*

Large areas of the north are covered with lush, tropical rain forest. The weather here is hot and wet all year round. But in the northeast there is very little rain, and the land is very dry.

▲ *A village in the northeast*

In southern Brazil, the summers (in January and February) are hot, but it gets very cold during the winter. Sometimes there is even snow.

The town of Florianópolis is built on an island. The island has beautiful lakes and beaches.

◀ *A spectacular waterfall in Canela, in southern Brazil*

▼ Gauchos *herd cattle on big farms in the south.*

8

"I love Florianópolis. The view from the top of this hill is fantastic!"—Lucas

At Home

Some of Brazil's cities are very big. In towns and cities most people live in small apartments or houses. Some people can afford big, luxurious apartments.

In villages along the northeast coast, most houses are made of wood. The weather is so warm that people are able to sleep outside in hammocks.

▲ Many people have hammocks outside their homes.

▶ In the cities there is a mixture of high-rise buildings and small houses.

◀ Houses in the south have thick walls, to keep people warm in the cold winters.

11

▲ *These houses have been built to look like Portuguese houses.*

About 500 years ago, Portuguese explorers landed in Brazil and took control of the country. They ruled Brazil for many years. Some of the houses that they built can still be seen today.

Lucas's father built their house, using wood and bricks. It has a fireplace, where the family can light fires to keep them warm during the winter.

▲ Like most other Brazilians, Lucas's family has color television.

"I like to play in my bedroom with my friends when it's too wet to play outside."—Lucas

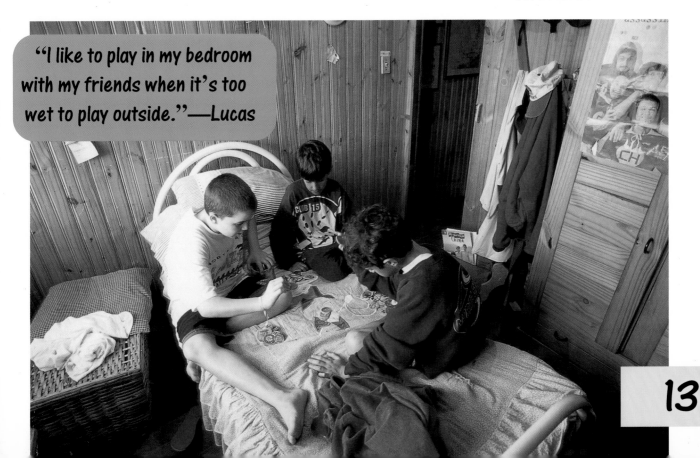

Brazilian Food

In northeastern Brazil, people eat a lot of seafood. In the south, the traditional food is *churrasco*—pieces of meat barbecued on metal sticks. The most famous Brazilian food is *feijoada*. It is a delicious mixture of black beans, spices, and different kinds of meat.

▲ Feijoada *is usually eaten with rice and sliced oranges.*

▶ *Lucas's family sometimes has lunch at the local youth club.*

"I always have *churrasco* at this restaurant—it's really delicious."—Mr. Neto

Many people buy their food in huge supermarkets, which are open twenty-four hours a day. Others visit local markets.

▲ *Colorful fruits at a market in northeast Brazil*

Lucas's family buys fish and seafood from the local fishermen. They eat lots of fresh fruits and vegetables, too, and drink water or fresh fruit juice.

▲ Lucas's mother cooks a special meal for Sunday lunch.

◄ Healthy salads are a favorite with all the family.

At Work

In the busy cities people work in banks, stores, and offices. Fishing and taking care of tourists are the main jobs in the north. Farming is important in central and southern Brazil. Many people work in the textile and car industries.

▼ A fisherman cuts up a huge fish he has just caught in the Amazon.

▲ Lucas's mother uses computers to keep in touch with her customers.

Lucas's mother works for a telecommunications company. His father produces programs for a television company.

"I sell sunglasses on the beach to tourists. It's very hot work!"—Mr. Silva

At School

▲ *Lucas goes to and from school by bus.*

▼ *Lucas meets some friends when he gets to school.*

Brazilian children start elementary school between the ages of five and six. In some areas, some children go to school in the morning, and others go in the afternoon.

Lucas goes to school in the morning. He wakes up at half-past six and has breakfast. He takes the bus to school with Renato. After school, he has to do his homework.

"Math is my favorite subject—aside from sports, of course!"—Lucas

Schools in the big cities are very modern. Children do some of their work on computers. In the country, classrooms are not usually so well equipped.

▼ *These girls are using the computers in their English class.*

◄ This large classroom in the north has big windows to keep the room cool.

Children play lots of sports. In the south, some schools have covered playgrounds so that the children can play sports even in the winter. The most popular games are soccer, volleyball, and basketball.

▼ Children playing soccer in an indoor playground

Free Time

Brazilian children really enjoy playing outside. There are many parks, beaches, and youth clubs where families can play sports together or just enjoy a picnic.

Lucas loves sports. He has karate lessons twice a week. Renato, his brother, is a very good surfer and is already a local champion.

▲ *Lucas goes swimming at the local pool every week.*

▼ *Lucas and his friends work on their surfboards.*

"The huge dunes near our house are great for sandboarding."—Lucas

Looking Ahead

Brazil has changed a lot in just a few years. New schools have been opened, especially in the northeast, so children can get a better education. New industries, such as telecommunications, provide different types of work for Brazilian people.

▲ *New airports have been built so that tourists can visit Brazil more easily.*

◀ *Even small towns have high-rise offices and apartments.*

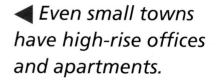

"When I grow up I want to be a karate teacher."—Lucas

Making Clay Models

Lucas likes to make models of animals from clay. The models he enjoys making most are dinosaurs. He leaves them in the hot summer sun until they are hard and dry.

- To make a dinosaur, you need a piece of clay about the size of your hand.

- Wet the clay until it becomes soft. Then roll it between your hands to make a sausage shape. Pull one end into a long point to make the tail.

▲ *Lucas rolls the clay to make a dinosaur.*

- At the other end, shape the clay into a round shape to make the head. Use a toothpick to make eyes and a mouth. Pinch and squeeze the clay under the body to make four legs.

- Leave your dinosaur in the sun until it is hard and dry, or ask an adult to bake it for you in the oven at low heat. Then paint it in your favorite colors.

◀ *Lucas with his dinosaur collection*

28

Brazil Fact File

▼ **Money Facts**

Brazilian money is the *real*. If you have more than one *real*, they are called *reais*. Two *reais* are about the same as $1. All the bills have pictures of an animal from the rain forest on one side.

▼ **The Brazilian Flag**

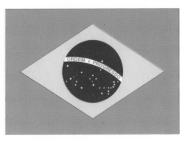

The three main colors on the flag have special meanings—green stands for the land and forest, yellow for gold, and blue for the sky.

Highest Peak

Brazil's highest mountain is called Pico da Bandeira. It is 9,495 ft. (3,014 m) high.

Soccer Fame

Brazil is the only country to have won the World Cup four times, and its most famous player, Pelé, has scored more than 1,000 goals. The Maracana Stadium in Rio de Janeiro is the biggest in the world and can hold 200,000 people.

▲ **River and Forest**

More water flows along the Amazon River than any other river in the world. The Amazon forest covers more than 2.3 million sq. mi. (6 million sq. km). It is the world's biggest rain forest.

▼ **Carnival**

Spectacular processions are held all over Brazil to celebrate Carnival. People in colorful costumes dance the famous Brazilian samba in the streets.

Glossary

Dunes Big heaps of sand on a beach.

Gauchos Cowboys of South America.

Hammocks Pieces of material with cords at each end, hung from the roof to make a bed.

Karate A sport in which two people fight, using their hands and feet, but no weapons.

Rain forest Thick forest that grows in tropical areas.

Sandboarding Sliding over sand dunes on a board.

Seafood Sea creatures such as shrimp or crabs, eaten as food.

Stilts Posts under a building that raise it off the ground.

Surfer Someone who rides over the waves on a board.

Telecommunications Communication at a distance, using machines such as telephones and computers that allow people to talk to each other, even though they are far apart.

Textile industry Factories that make cloth.

Tropical Between the Tropics of Cancer and Capricorn on the world map. Tropical areas have hot, wet weather all year round.

Further Information

Fiction:

Bender, Evelyn. *Brazil* (Major World Nations). New York: Chelsea House, 1998.

Carpenter, Mark L. *Brazil: An Awakening Giant*, revised edition (Discover Our Heritage). New York: Dillon Press, 1997.

Kent, Deborah. *Rio de Janeiro* (Cities of the World). Danbury, CT: Children's Press, 1996.

Lourie, Peter. *Amazon: A Young Reader's Look at the Last Frontier*. Honesdale, PA: Boyd's Mills Press, 1998.

Morrison, Marion. *Brazil* (Country Insights). Austin, TX: Raintree Steck-Vaughn, 1997.

Serra, Mariana. *Brazil* (Food and Festivals). Austin, TX: Raintree Steck-Vaughn, 1999.

Useful Addresses

Brazilian Embassy
3400 International Drive NW
Washington, DC 20008

Brazilian Consulate General
3810 Wilshire Blvd.
Los Angeles, CA 90010

Index

All the numbers in **bold** refer to illustrations.